The Lost Language of Shadows

David Olsen

First Edition 2022

David Olsen has asserted his authorship and given permission to
Dempsey & Windle for these poems to be published here.

Published by Dempsey & Windle
15 Rosetrees
Guildford
Surrey
GU1 2HS
UK
01483 571164
dempseyandwindle.com

A catalogue record for this book is available from the British Library

British Library Cataloguing-in-Publication Data

ISBN: 978-1-913329-85-3

Printed and bound in the UK

Contents

Dramatis Personae

The Lost Language of Shadows

With gratitude, as always, to:

Paul Surman, my first reader
Cathy Young
Hanne Busck-Nielsen
Ellen MacDonald-Kramer
Anne Hammond
Carolyn Moseley
Gwilym Scourfield
Heather and Roger Burt
Byron Brown

Dramatis Personae

Double Bill

Randolph Scott was twice my height
when a child's ticket cost 20 cents
and a bag of popcorn was a dime.

The Movietone newsreel was first
(propaganda about a war somewhere),
then the A feature (often women's fare
with twin beds, kissing and tears),
and a Looney Tunes or Disney cartoon.
Last came the B picture, usually
a western to satisfy a man's thirst
for action, or lust for adventure.

I rode on cattle drives from Texas
to the railhead somewhere north,
chewed popcorn from the chuck wagon
while a campfire flickered nearby,
or worried through gunfights when
the white hat's six-gun never ran out
and black hats' shots always missed.
A pretty woman might be in peril
from wild Indians or Mexican rustlers.
A blood feud about a dead brother
might motivate the plot. Through it all,
Randolph Scott stood lean and tall.

And still grown men re-enact frontier
heroics in Stetson hats and boots
with high heels and pointed toes,
carry guns, and vote Republican.

L'Heure Bleue

In post-war years my mother
dabbed Evening in Paris cologne
from a bottle of deepest blue,
while radio ads for Guerlain's
L'Heure Bleue promised romance,
conjured that hushed, suspended time
when lovers await the first star.

At 12, I languished in hospital,
waiting for reluctant bones to heal,
waiting for relief from the itch
of months within the plaster cast.
On clear nights, tall windows
and fanlights across the ward
framed a pure indigo sky –
that still recalls *l'heure bleue*.

Corn Broom

Nowadays it's hard to buy one;
in city shops there's nothing but
push brooms with plastic bristles.
I found my broom in a country store
that sold some of this, some of that,
everything simple lives might need.

When the business end gets ragged,
I even it up with scissors. Like new.

While the aroma of baking bread
wafts through the house, I hear
a sandpaper swish over kitchen lino.
I dig the broom into the corners,
squeeze it into that narrow space
behind the fridge. I herd bits
of dried food overlooked by the dog
toward the centre of the floor.
Bending reluctant knees, I stoop
to wield the dustpan, think of Mum.
How sweeping was a ritual,
a communion with her instrument,
like Casals with his cello. Once
I asked her why she worked so hard.
To something the size of a cockroach,
a toast crumb looks like a T-bone steak.

The Half Eagle

While confined to a hospital bed,
Mum prayed for a miracle cure,
placing faith in modern science
and, equally, an ancient myth.

Her brother, distrusting the state
and fiat currency, believed in gold.
He produced a five-dollar gold coin –
a half eagle minted in the last century,
and inscribed In God We Trust –
with a golden bezel and chain, to hold
warm healing gold close to pale skin.

When her state became so dire
it was clear she wouldn't survive,
as her only brother, he told her
she wouldn't leave her bed alive.
A truth, however unwelcome,
a gift of gold.

Under the Madrone

Despite owning a nickel-plated .38,
Les fled Oakland for fear of assault,
and retired to southern Oregon.
He bought a few acres where
a bungalow lay low under limbs
of an evergreen madrone whose
red bark peeled off to expose
a satin sheen of silver-green,
as if the tree possessed the spirit
of an alluring woman who tantalized
by slowly shedding her gown.

Beneath the myrtle and madrone,
Les contended with gophers for dominion
over a garden of golden poppy,
Indian paintbrush, lupine, larkspur
and reluctant roses. Eyes weak
from decades of fine print, he read little,
dispelled loneliness with Ancient Age,
and began to believe that little people
occupied the closet of his spare room.

His only son, Herb, who'd moved nearby
with a second wife, Ida – a greedy harpy
who prodded her husband to claim
his inheritance before the fact –
watched his father slide, become unfit
to manage his everyday affairs.

When the old man learned that control
of his assets had been usurped, he phoned
Herb to say he would shoot him, though
he never acted on the threat. When Les
became incontinent, Ida called him
a nasty, filthy man for the messes
he made. He didn't last long after that.

Container

Our cottonwoods were shedding leaves
as the flat-bed truck backed onto the drive.
Soon a march of household goods would fill
the half-container for the voyage to England,
and an unknown destination in Oxford.

A couple of days hence, you would oversee
your goods as men packed a moving van
for the trek west to California. Both aware
that we would occupy smaller quarters,
we'd sold or donated unneeded furniture,

so the residue might fit. The sun rose high,
and still the men loaded the container until
every space was filled with tables and chairs
and cardboard cartons of records and books,
cameras and kitchen pans, towels and sheets.

I signed and initialled papers; the driver
and crew climbed into the cab and started
the diesel engine. Without looking back,
they pulled away, and I was left by myself,
abandoned with finality, bereft and alone.

Rondo for Red Hawk

Your womb-grip was tenuous
and you emerged too soon. On
worried winter nights I crept in
your room to hear your sleeping breath.

While I drove us home from Death
Valley you went all white and wan.
In hospital you were transfused
and endured a dozen daily
blood-count pricks. As mysteriously
as internal bleeding began, it ceased.

When that madwoman attacked you
with a rocking chair, I restrained
her while she struggled against me
and the demons that possessed her.

At Silver Lake we Indian Guides
went sledding. Mishap of momentum
sent my Red Hawk toward the strut
of an idling snowmobile, but
another boy of nine, a brave
goalkeeper, braced then made the save.

Hiking with Sierra Club friends,
you ran ahead and froze in the road
before a moving car. My heart stopped,
as did the driver in slivered time.

When pavement's edge ripped a tyre
from its rim and you wanted
to give up driving there and then,
I gulped and said to try again.

Repeated passing wears a path.
You now await your golden first;
two decades hence, at last you'll know
how hard it's been, the letting go.

Symmetry

Chess is not like life; chess is life.
~Bobby Fischer

Son, you never liked my openings.
I see in your eyes that you despise
the Four Knights, but I admire
its fearful symmetry:
the tense reflection until white
or black chooses loneliness.

Remember your first win?
Hyperventilating,
you were up a rook
and about to burn
a heretical bishop.
Damned if I gave up,

I would not concede.
I awaited a blunder,
but you survived the errors
of ferocious youth
and mate you did,
new king of the castle.

I now decline all even trades,
prolong the middle game,
repulse a reckless
rampaging queen.
Even as white
I defend.

At this perilous hour
it's dawn with seconds.
Your pawn's move
reflects mine
in ritual perfection:
our harlequin minuet.

Suspension
San Francisco, 17 October 1989

The World Series is suspended
before the first pitch.
Candlestick Park survives the jolt,
but screens go blank.

Night tiptoes in.
Powerless, we light candles,
turn on a battery radio.

A newscaster reads of fires
in the Marina – her neighbourhood –
unaware of the state of her home.

Reports of damage trickle in:
a section of the Bay Bridge has collapsed;
in Oakland a triple-layer interchange pancaked,
crushing drivers in their cars;
a brick wall smashed a bookshop cafe
in Santa Cruz.

We go to bed,
seeking the comfort of candles,
quaking at every aftershock.

Snow!

I peer outside and discover a chastened road,
a morning of bridal innocence where
no wheels have rutted the illusion,
and a lone fool plods under an umbrella,
like a clown with parasol and bulbous shoes.

I think of how you – now uncaring miles
away – once prayed for a carefree day
while nibbling peanut butter toast, and bent
toward the radio for news of which schools
would close, in hopes of a career on your
Flexible Flyer, and a snow angel's afterlife.

I think of how our separate but shared
experiences of snow brought us together
when I described the Zen of clearing fluff
from driveway and path before the clang
and scrape of the city's plough churned up
ice and salted grit to the foot of the driveway,
and ruined the peace of the feathered night.

Binding Wounds

A smudge of rust corrodes
a dressing wrap, as drying blood
infuses layered gauze.
Unrolling mesh reveals
in every wind a wider stain,
as a hidden wound's exposed.

A bruise affronts in present time
but, like healing turns of gauze,
each spooling year absorbs
the ooze from seeping hurts.
A scar persists at memory's edge,
but fades to faint irrelevance.

Communion

Two kites intersect in a Venn
diagram of separate gyres.

We turn north from the river,
amble toward the terrace house,

reluctant to end our break
and resume the work.

The glory of the cherry tree
outside our study window

comes into view. We open the gate,
step lightly through the snowflakes

on the path, feel falling petals
bestowing butterfly kisses.

Indoors, we climb narrow stairs
and take our seats, side by side.

In the cherry tree a starling fidgets;
months will pass before ovaries

become fruit. We settle to write
in companionable silence, each

circling words worthy of the day.

Equinox

Serrated cherry leaves ignite
their slow curling burn.
In your glowing solstice,
your days prolonged,
freshened spring has passed.
In maturity you consolidate
gains, gather sunlight for a ripe
harvest of sweetened fruit.
Your glories lie ahead;
mine are memories
you're helping to preserve.

My day is balanced by night.

The blade of the wind is keen,
and soon golden leaves
will rip from every branch,
cower against the garden wall,
and moulder to blackened dust.

Our tree, bared to its bones,
will bear the winter in trust
that other summers will come.

Our Bench

Our favourite outdoor perch
wasn't ours, exactly; it stood
in the botanic garden beneath
a timeless copper beech, though
we liked to think it was ours
alone. Here we shared private
moments in this public space.

And here we contemplated
the wisdom of tulips and daffodils
in spring, and of resigned autumn
leaves forced from untenable
positions by foreknowing buds,
leaving numberless tiny scars
to overwinter while your knowing
fingers entwined mine.

Murmuration

A breathing cloud of starlings,
reflected in momentary mirrors,
flickers in wanton trickery,

alters a collective mind
in hive unison, as if reversal
itself is the purpose of all.

Indecision or contradiction
buffets me in winds
of your capricious whim.

To escape the suspense
of randomness, I depart
in deference to indifference.

Fettuccine Alfredo

I grate a drift of *grana padano*,
dice an onion with sharp tears,
and melt butter in stainless steel
that reflects a fretted face.
In another pan I heat water
for pasta; grains of salt provoke
a fury of boiling. To the butter
and onion I add double cream
and stir in the cheese.

The sauce tastes as it always did
when folded into tender semolina,
but the missing ingredient is joy.
Once our favourite comfort food,
our Sunday sacrament is today
only starch and fat.

Before Me a Desert

With your usual grace
you tell me
Move on, as I've done.

Easy for you.
You're the exemplar
of how to move on.
That hot August night
you moved on with obscene ease,
bedazzled by prestidigitation:

fleeting touch of lips,
glancing brush of breast,
calculated testing,
before his bold decisive grope,
leading you to move on
to desecration of your temple.

Devoted to your care,
I'd held nothing back,
never intending to move on.
Now you tell me
Take care of yourself.
Move on.

Before me a desert.
I have neither map
nor reliable compass,
and no clear destination
beyond a bare horizon.

Spring Blush

Alan's ghost was everywhere in her Oxford house.
Hundreds of hours of sweat equity left his touch;
wallpaper stripped, walls sanded and filled,
then Spring Blush emulsion paint warmed
the stairwell, hall, and bed- and reception rooms.
He had done her bedroom first, to provide
a refuge from the chaos in the rest of the house.

In a Summertown gallery he had found
an elegant glass vase, clear with a rose swirl –
the perfect accent to complement the décor.
When she unwrapped the gift, she took it straight
to the bedroom and centred it on the dresser –
exactly the place he'd intended, as if to affirm
the consonance of their vision and taste
blooming in the colour scheme of every room.

After her conference fling became a long-
distance affair, Alan's banishment failed to dispel
reminders of his presence, and it was a relief
when she moved to a university in the southeast.
This time she paid for renovation of her new home:
the same bathroom tile, similar hardwood flooring,
and Spring Blush throughout. She felt settled
when the rose-swirl vase took its appointed place.

A Trick of the Light

While washing up,
my hands in warm froth,
from the corner of my eye
I glimpsed you.

Always the practical one,
you would say it was
a trick of the light
glinting off my glasses.

Then tell me how
I can still feel your hand
burning, burning
through Harris Tweed
when you touched my sleeve
that first time.

And tell me why, years later,
I can still smell the essence
of your hair in my shampoo.

After velvet curtains closed,
and you became a wisp
of spirit-smoke
rising, rising
to interment in the sky,

can you deny me now
the truth of morning light?

Awake from Five

Her constant face swims
from the nightstand photograph,
as if from a tray of developer
under a safelight's vigilant gaze.

The lightening room conjures
blue sparks from intent eyes,
quick slim fingers on a keyboard,
cappuccino cooling nearby.

Unwell

in a sleeping room of static familiars:
December memory frozen in a frame,
guitar untouched atop the wardrobe,
bookcase of remaindered paperbacks
in silent reproach. Apart from the clock's
slow numerals, all is a constant tinnitus
unworthy of notice and best ignored.

The window's a rhombus of pallid air –
a backlit bird with urgent intent
passing too fast to introduce itself,
the entropy of dispersing contrails
expressing a tiring universe destined
to stillness. A stylus wakes the fluid sky –
purposeful people going somewhere.

Heart Trouble

She'd inherited her Dad's small feet
and weak heart.

She predicted her own demise
with the insouciance

of a weather forecaster
interpreting isobars

and highs and lows
of pressure, temperature,

states of mind:
It'll be the old ticker.

The other day a friend
sent a link to an obituary

from the local paper,
with condolences.

But all that was so long ago.
She made her choice.

Brutal time had cooled
a searing passion to a shrug.

Checking for Mail

Sturdy boots crunch through a crust
of fresh snow on the curving drive.
My goal is the arch of galvanized
sheet metal mounted on a post
within the postman's reach
when seated in his blue and white
motor vehicle, not quite a car,
not quite a jeep or small truck.

I pull down the front flap to find
the usual assortment of envelopes
with windows and things to pitch
into recycling, unread. The rolled
local paper's in the cylindrical
metal tube below the box.
As usual, nothing personal today.

I pause to listen to a bird perched
among the styli of bare birches
engraving the pewter sky, imagining
that, beyond the curve of my road,
someone has left a warm kitchen
to brave the cold and check for mail
without expectation, but with hope.

The unruly glass

fails to learn
for lack of memory.

Every lesson is strange,
encountered for the first time

with the surprise
of revelation.

There is no past or future,
just a timeless glance

or enigmatic succession
of dying instants.

The reversed image
confounds the self-portrait.

A surly servant
of the insecure and the vain,

the insubordinate glass
betrays master or mistress,

inflicts discomfort on those
unable to bear contradiction,

or deludes the self
with approximate truth.

Sixth Chair

after 'The Violinist' by Constantin Piliuţă
(Romanian, 1929-2003)

The second violin section
now comprises just five chairs.
Sixth chair blames austerity,
not arthritis and clouded sight.

Each morning, he picks up
his instrument case and leaves
the flat he shares with his wife
of 40 years. She believes

he's rehearsing, while he hopes,
like Micawber, that something
will turn up. To occupy his days
he rides a bus to a remote café,

eats nothing to conserve funds
and delay his confession.
Sloe gin eases his plight.
Familiar strains of Brahms

da capo through his mind.
Only finger memory remains.
His instrument case is empty;
the violin's been sold.

Residues

At 96, the pianist had outlived friends
she wouldn't have recognized.

Her only daughter stifles tears,
accepts the arm of her confidante.

Seated behind, a distant cousin
and a nurse from the care home.

At the rear, rented pallbearers
sing with practised confidence.

The hired minister fumbles names.
A burgundy curtain parts, closes

on remains smoothly conveyed.
Spirit-smoke. Ashes. Release.

Ambivalent embrace
of reluctant freedom.

Understudy

Six nights and two matinees a week,
I watch her.

I study how she turns,
lifts an eyebrow a millimetre,
lowers her voice to command attention,
creates tension with stillness.

I'm prettier, though not quite as tall.
I have few entrances, fewer lines.
No one notices me in my maid's uniform –
black with white apron and flat shoes.

But I know all her lines.
I'm ready, just in case.
In case of what? A cold? Flu?
Not likely. She's strong.
Never misses a performance.
Famous for it.
A reliable evening star, like Venus.

But when a well-wisher tells her
Break a leg...
I live in hope.

The Balcony
Île Saint-Louis, Paris

I turn away from temptation
in the window of a *pâtisserie*.
Something makes me look up
at the building opposite – perhaps
the weight of someone's gaze.

A young woman sits in the tall
open window of her apartment,
her foot on the iron grille.
She's taking the morning sun
while reading the paper.

In a mood of presumed kinship,
I imagine it's *Le Monde*
or *Libération*, not *Le Figaro*.
She nods to me; I return
her gesture of mutual regard.

This, and her tawny blond hair,
suggest she might be American,
maybe taking a language course
at *L'Alliance Française*,
or studying at the Sorbonne.

Venn diagrams of separate lives
intersect tangentially for a moment.
I wonder if she might be homesick,
or revelling in her little corner
of this world city we both love.

She will turn the page,
and I will go on my wistful way,
pleased by the happy accident
of an encounter of no immediate
import or lasting consequence.

Aboard the Idle Mind Express

As others, anxious over keyboards,
stroke their memoranda and reports,
I feel a passing twinge of guilt
while flipping junk-food pages filled

with handbags, hosiery and holidays.
I set aside the empty calories
and read instead unrolling scrolls
as frost descends on slumping hills.

The ground is bare of corn and hops;
the land is in repose. The crops
are in, the fields fallow in their turn,
and cattle slumber in the barn.

It comforts me to ponder that,
like grass from quiescent earth,
the most arresting thought
arises from a rested mind.

My sympathetic breathing slows
to that of a sleeping love
or daydreaming land that knows
there's nothing more to prove.

The Lost Language of Shadows

Flora of Arras

i.m. Edward Thomas (1878-1917)

Whose farm was this, where alien shoots
were mired in trouble?
Who bent the stems, then sliced them off,
cut them down to stubble?

Who sowed the grass with rusting coils
of rootless rambling vines
and tended them with tractors
of such bizarre designs?

A reckless ploughman wasted seeds
and scattered all around
the tender cultivated buds
now mouldering underground.

Duty of Care

Bayeux War Cemetery, Normandy

Not far from the breathing saline sea,
apple orchards, and yellow rapeseed fields,
rise perfect ranks of cream-coloured stones,
as if dressed right and at attention for roll-call.
The monuments, darkened by the stain of rain,
bear the regimental seal and name, rank,
and dates of each combatant, some graced
with a grieving mother's adoring phrase.
Others are inscribed: *Known Unto God*

Nearby, the Bayeux Memorial commemorates
1,808 men with no known grave.

Thousands of these had drilled in uniform rows,
then endured months of dread and hours of chaos.
For them, order is restored. In this peaceful space,
wisteria flowers bow from archways, while stately
sentinel-trees shade the sharp boundaries between
grass and perennial beds at the foot of each stone.
Like medics and nurses fulfilling humanity's bond,
gardeners tend the wounded earth with a duty of care.

Passchendaele Farm

And there, in the midst of it all,
near slender second-growth
poplars dressed with healing green,
a plough peels curling waves
of earth to yield an ominous clank.

A century of freeze and thaw
has expelled another artillery
shell from unforgiving ground
where men drowned in mud,
leaving skulls amid the shells.

A fifth of shells fired with clockwork
regularity failed to explode, and men
where duds fell counted themselves
among the fortunate few. Yet after
so long, still the shells could kill.

The farmer makes a routine call,
summons a disposal crew to disarm
the dormant shell at a safe remove,
and ploughs on through earth
unnaturally fertile and black.

Resettlement to Koidanov

German-occupied Belorussia, 1943

Here, outside Minsk, trains disgorge
those promised a new and better life.
On arrival, they are given receipts
for their belongings to confirm
their belief that they will be reunited
with their goods when they reach
their new home in a village
just beyond the forest.

After a journey without sanitation,
the people are ordered to strip.
Out of sight, the clothes
are searched for paper money,
diamonds, or gold coins. The new
arrivals don't become restive
until dentists from the ghetto
begin extracting gold crowns.

The few who try to run are shot.
Others, in groups of 20, are herded
to the edge of a freshly dug pit
the size of a swimming pool.
Mothers tell children to hold still,
as men in field grey, and officers
in black, hold pistols to the back
of each head. When our supply
of Jews is exhausted for the day,
in the barracks, for every bullet,
a full bottle of vodka is consumed.

Hunger
Northern Ireland, 1981

The night awaits the snow.
The night yearns for gauze
to embalm the ancient crime
and wrap the naked scars
from the grinding stone of time.

The night awaits the snow.
Clouds of chilled silence billow
through gun-metal blue bars
that give teeth to the window
and bound the errant stars.

Silence hungers for snow.
Barring bread from this keep,
your mistress now is Pain
who admits no earthly sleep;
your silence cries again.

Your bones await the snow
beneath imported blanket wool.
Within the walls of grim Long Kesh,
a belly strangely full,
your liver sucks the jellied flesh.

The blanket-men watch for snow
through slits in H-Block walls,
lament denied family cloaks
like naked beaten Gaels
on slabs beneath sacred oaks.

Ireland prays for snow.
You observe the ancient Irish rite
of fasting at the landlord's gate,
confront the rule of might
with will and Celtic fate.

The night pleads for snow.
The Armalite and a mother's pleas
alike to no avail,
while sense is lost in memories
and hope avoids this pale.

Snow comes at last like stars
outcast from the firmament.
Your uncommended soul alone
enfolds presentiment
as the grave embraces bone.

Perigee

10 August 2014

The bemused moon bends to hear
a Babel of tribal dialects and tongues
summoning the sons of Abraham
to their unerring, righteous cause –
the One True God will destroy
the false creed of infidels –
as feral orphans root in rubbled streets
and ancient blood lines surge
across arbitrary lines in the sand.

Bystanders ignore cyclonic floods
and rising tides, while elsewhere
scorching winds parch the earth,
desiccating leaf and grain.
Wildfires rage as hapless states –
paralyzed by dogmatic strife
and debts to untaxed private wealth –
cannot act, unless by reckless means.

On the Street a moon-maddened fiddler
twists his tuning pegs to raise the pitch.
He plies his frenzied bow, unmindful
of overstressed strings destined to break.

The moon retreats to apogee.

A Bedouin Welcome

A visitor is always welcome
to water, food, and shelter
inside a Bedouin tent.

Pounding sun and blowing sand,
desiccating heat and thirst
threaten life; hospitality

is a necessity for survival.
The host knows the next time,
it could be he who needs help.

The desert Muslim knows
when desperate people ask
to be let in, that they may live,

he must find room in the tent,
provide shelter, dignity, a sense
of home for a brother in distress.

Caddy

Lake Chabot Golf Course, Oakland, 1930s

In the Great Depression – the one before
the Great Recession 80 years later –
my Dad was a caddy. He carried the bag
and clubs of men who were well off,
even after the Wall Street Crash of '29.

They weren't busted in the Dust Bowl,
had means to buy when distressed
assets passed from weak hands to strong.
In the midst of the trough, they bought
cheaply, while those without real jobs
lacked capital or access to credit,
could buy nothing of lasting worth.

Some, like Dad, were rented serfs,
servants for a sunny afternoon;
they were left holding the bag.

Underground Economy

I take refuge from harsh autumn wind
in a charity shop. Despite bedside
stacks of unread books at home,
I still indulge a harmless addiction;
too much is never enough.

Shelves bestow their treasures;
I take spy thrillers to the counter
and wait my turn. Ahead of me, a man
in rundown trainers and dungarees
with holes in the knees is about to pay.

He's chosen slacks and brown leather shoes,
a presentable shirt and tasteful tie.
He folds them carefully and slides them
into a paper bag, then pulls out a thin
wallet and pays with a debit card.

I suspect he may be facing a job
interview or appearance in court.
He steps out the door into a frenzy
of fallen leaves. To respect his dignity,
I refrain from calling out *Good luck.*

Night Express

I plod the Paddington platform,
too weary to walk farther
than the nearest carriage door.
All the forward-facing seats are full;
I'm resigned to riding backwards,
competing for space for my feet.

Fatigue is revealed in every face.
All appear to have worked late –
or will say they did – and may
expect a meal from the microwave.
Those with a residue of ambition
open laptops or shuffle papers;
others fuss with phones or slump
in Great Western's soiled seats.
One opens a nip of Johnny Walker.

With a jolt we are under way.
Watching through my ghostly
half-reflection in the window,
I see retaining walls tagged
with signatures of the voiceless,
terraces enduring noise and smoke,
and stations along the milk run
or those abandoned for Efficiency.

The disgorge at Slough allows
a change of seats. On to Reading.
A great exchange takes place;
nearly as many get on as off.
Then to Oxford, the end of the line,
the terminus. *All change, please.*

Paying Attention
Montmartre, Paris

Concentrate. Money's at stake.
A man shuffles three counters,
one marked on the underside.
Shell game. Pull out your wallet.
Put up €10. You win. Easy money.
Smirk at one or two nearby idlers.
Double or nothing? Sure. Why not?
Bet your tenner plus his.
Now, pay even closer attention.
Watch those hands. Watch them.
What? You lose. A fluke.
Bored onlookers melt away.
You can beat this chump.
Reach for your wallet. Gone.

Blood Orange Sky
Pacific Northwest

Beneath a heat dome
ranging over several states,
dry winds whipped flames
through parched crowns
of desiccated spruce and fir.

Along the Columbia Gorge,
around Puget Sound,
and throughout the Palouse,
people fled for their lives,
leaving their homes to burn.

Wildfires are commonplace,
but these were unlike
anything seen in the vast
blackened countryside
under a nightmare sky.

Wildfire, Big Basin

Boulder Creek, Santa Cruz Mountains, California

I was eight when Grandpa showed me redwoods.
The Mother of the Forest reached above 300 feet.
A cross-section of trunk, propped against a boulder,
was wider than Grandpa could spread his arms:
a wheel too large for any wagon I'd ever seen.
I fed a deer and felt the rasp of its rough tongue.

Thunderstorms and lightning were once rare
in our dry air, but altered weather and years
of drought created vast swathes of tinder.
Lightning strikes ignited hundreds of fires.
Here one raged among madrones, firs and oaks,
where redwoods had seen two thousand springs.

Now the air is thick with smoke. The forest floor's
littered with flaming branches; fallen trees block
the park road. Some redwoods are down,
but will sprout anew from burls, as reclining logs
have done since Roman times. Cinnamon bark,
rich in tannin – to repel pests and retard fire –
preserves this primeval forest for another
small boy to stand at the base of a spire
and tilt his head, and gaze up. No, higher.

En Passant

Moist tropical air
once condensed over cool waters;
fog dripped from leaves to shallow roots.
Stasis of millennia:
patient evolution
in perfect harmony with seasons.

Then drought.

Sentinels comprehend,
but cannot speak,
except among themselves
through intertwined roots.

In the west
zinc thickens to lead.
Light shifts toward yellow.
Wind rises.
The sky cracks
with rebounding light.

Dry inland grass ignites.
Embers ride the wind.
Drivers flee burning homes
on clogged roads,
perish with their photographs.

Petri Dish

Nutrients abound in a petri dish.
A few introduced microbes
multiply by dividing.
Thriving in ideal ambience,
numbers rise by powers of two,
spread across available space.

Growth reaches the edge,
but still organisms pile up,
each stratum striving to survive,
all individuals competing
for dwindling resources.

Meanwhile, excreted waste
accumulates where there's
nowhere safe to isolate it;
toxic remains sicken and kill
succeeding generations.
The once-rich culture dies.

Mnemonics

Inscribed granites outlast and atone
for the memories they signify.
Yet ice cleaves the stone;
rain and grief erode it and lay
the crumbled silt as corrupted
shale to be folded and subducted
into the underworld's
molten convective swirl.

Persistent as ageless guilt,
magma probes to find a flaw,
then penetrates the fault
to outcrop anew
as feldspar and quartz
with grains as fine or coarse
as the men they will edify.
So much, then, for eternity.

Uncharted

No North Star. No satnav or maps.
No charts of perilous shoals
or submerged reefs or rocks
aspiring to atolls or isles.

No foghorns or lighthouses pierce
the dark to warn of the wreckage
of indifferent drift. While mooring
lines slip from cleats of memory,

a forgettable wake is swamped
by the groundswell's enduring
pulse of a heart beyond reach.

What remains of us is a logbook
of delusions and self-serving lies
with a truthful last page left blank.

Notes

'Rondo for Red Hawk': Red Hawk is the Native American name my son chose for his YMCA Indian Guides alias.

'Symmetry': In the Four Knights game, after three moves by each player, the positions are mirror images.

'Suspension': The earthquake described is known as the Loma Prieta.

'Resettlement to Koidanov': The events of this poem are described in *Ostland*, by David Thomas.

Acknowledgements

The following poems appeared in the journal, anthology, or chapbook cited:

Acumen: 'Double Bill'
Ash & Bones: 'Duty of Care'
The Deronda Review: 'Unwell'
Elusions: Refugee Poems, WaterWood Press anthology: 'A Bedouin Welcome'
Envoi: 'Binding Wounds'
Exit Wounds, Finishing Line Press chapbook: 'Fettuccine Alfredo' and
    'Before Me a Desert'
The French Literary Review: 'The Balcony', '*L'Heure Bleue*' and
    'Sixth Chair'
Gold Dust: 'Uncharted'
Greatest Hits 1983-2000, Pudding Publications chapbook in an invitational
    series: 'Hunger' won First Prize in the 1989 Daly City poetry competition.
From Hallows to Harvest, Cinnamon Press competition anthology: 'Equinox'
The Interpreter's House: 'Mnemonics' was commended in the Bedford Prize
    Competition.
Magma: 'Wildfire, Big Basin'
Months to Years: 'Residues'

No, Achilles: War Poetry, WaterWood Press anthology: 'Flora of Arras'
OpenDoor: 'Murmuration' and 'Under the Madrone'
Pedestal: 'Petri Dish'
Poetry News: 'Paying Attention'
ROPES (National University of Ireland – Galway): 'Rondo for Red Hawk'
Tranquility, Kind of a Hurricane Press anthology: 'Our Bench'

'Symmetry' was commended in the Cannon Poets Silver Jubilee National Competition.
'Aboard the Idle Mind Express' was shortlisted in the *Countryside Tales* Winter Competition.

Also by David Olsen

Unfolding Origami
(Cinnamon Press 2015)

Past Imperfect
(Cinnamon Press 2019)

After Hopper & Lange
(Oversteps Books 2021)

Nocturnes
(Dempsey & Windle 2021)

Poetry chapbooks from US publishers include *Exit Wounds* (2017), *Sailing to Atlantis* (2013), *New World Elegies* (2011), and *Greatest Hits* (2001).